Natives of Eternity

by

Flower A. Newhouse

Other books by Flower A. Newhouse

Touched by Angels
Angels of Nature
Kingdom of the Shining Ones
Insights into Reality
Songs of Deliverance
The Armor of the Spiritual Life
Seven Bodies Unveiled
Disciplines of the Holy Quest
The Collected Works series: Christian Mysticism,
Esoteric Teachings, Disciplines

Biography of Flower A. Newhouse

Songs from the House of Pilgrimage
by Dr. Stephen Isaac

Cover Illustration: A Race Spirit of Venus

Much of this content was originally written in 1937.

ISBN-13: 978-0910378345
ISBN-10: 0910378347

Dedicated

to Humanity, whose Eternal Quest

is boundless

An Angel of the Morning

CONTENTS

Natives of Eternity

INTRODUCTION

The benefit or pleasure which we receive from the reading of a book or the contemplation of any created work depends very largely upon the attitude in which we approach it. In order to receive help or inspiration from an artist or author we must first of all let down the barriers which we so often build between ourselves and our fellows, for, just as we cannot see the beauties of a landscape unless we open our eyes, neither can we appreciate and utilize spiritual help unless we are prepared to stretch forth our hands to the Teacher and so establish that certain "rapport" through which all true inspiration is conveyed from one soul to another.

Such a condition is especially necessary in the case of such a truly marvellous revelation as is contained in the following pages. To approach these fascinating chapters in a mood of casual interest, or mild indifference or mere curiosity will be to forfeit entirely the priceless blessings which they contain. In this book the circumstances are but the frame and the characters portrayed are but the background for the experiences in the inner worlds of existence, which are not objective ideas to be examined by the intellect but rather living realities, intended to become potent influences in the daily life of the reader.

To know that these Great Souls do exist, in close contact with struggling humanity, should excite in us something more than passing interest or pious wonder. It should mean a tremendous renewal of our individual courage and determination to fit ourselves to join with Them in Their mighty work. To associate ourselves with Them, even though it be unconsciously at first, will be seen both as a priceless privilege and as a sublime objective to be kept before us every moment of our lives.

To the author, who, by the perfection of her own living accomplishment has won for herself direct contact with these "Natives of Eternity" and who has had the courage to pass on to a weary world these wonderful glimpses of the glories in which she would have us share, will go the deep gratitude and love of all who read these pages with receptive minds and open hearts.

JAMES R. GERARD

FOREWORD

One of the most blessed realizations that can come to any person is the one which enables them to know of the countless lives that exist about them invisible to their outer senses. Human beings are but a single manifestation of the Infinite Creator. Beside them are hosts of ascending Forms intent upon final unification within the spirit of the Eternal Maker. To learn of these myriad expressions of God's life, adds breadth, depth and loftiness to our thoughts. Our present efforts are concerned with the building of character and the use of those principles which harmonize, heal and advance our beings. The added knowledge of Lives progressing side by side with us is inwardly enriching and gladdening.

The Angels are just as fully a part of my consciousness as are my family and friends. The most inspired moments I have experienced were in Their company. The Masters have imparted all that is embodied in these teachings. The Angels have been the "Bright Messengers," channels of tender, sacred and joyous benedictions. This faculty of extended vision which permits me to see the Radiant Ones becomes useful only when I share its perceptions with others. This volume is written with the purpose of bringing Them more closely and understandingly into the hearts of persons whom They are striving to reach. My prayer is that Their love and nearness will be felt by those who read these pages.

IN EXPLANATION OF THE ILLUSTRATIONS

A natural question which arises in the minds of those who study the pictures included in this volume, is, "Are these Faces idealistic conceptions of Angels or are they authentic likenesses?" They are embodied in this text *only* because these illustrations are accurate resemblances of the types of Beings mentioned in this volume.

With gratitude we wish to acknowledge the kindness of the artist, Miss Mildred Compton, for the use of her creative perceptions. Her entrance in our lives was an answer to a prayer I had in my heart for several years. Since teaching about Angelic forms, I have longed to meet a sincere, sensitive channel who could illustrate on paper or canvas true descriptions of these Radiant Ones. Miss Compton has glimpses of these Beings at times when she is in a very high state of attunement. She is not always aware of the kind of Life she discerns. Each of the paintings she has brought forth, that I have seen, represents a definite Server or Order.

This volume is an announcement of revelations that we trust to continue at length throughout the years.

FLOWER A. NEWHOUSE

THE KINGDOM OF THE ANGELS

Strange wonders permeate our world, sublime mysteries almost too pure for our full understanding. Our planet, and its atmosphere, is not only pervaded by invisible radioactive waves and silent, potent rays, but by shining beings whose ceaseless ministries enliven and uplift us. More wonderful than the far-reaching effects of television, or the harnessing of the inimitable cosmic rays, will be our recognition of these glorious presences. Since time unfurled its amazing creation, Angelic Beings have nurtured the advancement and unfoldment of humanity. References to them have usually been accepted with amusement and disbelief. Behind every ageless belief, however, lies a hidden reality whose meaning should be sought with earnestness. Our ignorance of Angels does not make them nonexistent, it only closes us to their existence. Our yearning to realize them opens us to their association.

The Angelic Kingdom, like the human kingdom, is a path of evolving life. It is composed of beings whose bodies, compared to ours, are etheric. The purpose underlying Angelic unfoldment is perfection through joyousness and service. The human way is impelled toward the development of love and wisdom. Those who inhabit the celestial kingdom are free from strife and evil. Human beings are strengthened by their overcoming the forces of discord and malice within themselves. Angels are immortal; human beings require the rest of death to prepare them for new cycles of self-expression.

The way of Angelic evolution is exacting and long, whereas that of human wayfarers, though strenuous, is comparatively short. The more individuals associate with nature, the purer their vibrations, because nature beings have no destructive emotions. All is done consciously from the highest and purest levels.

There are numerous celestial orders, many of which we know very little about. The groups from whom we receive ministrations are:

1. The Angels of Nature
2. The Builders of Form
3. The Angels of Inspiration
4. The Angels of Love
    a. Guardian Angels
    b. Healing Angels
    c. Religious Angels
    d. Song Angels
5. The Angels of Birth and Death

The Angels devoted to nature cause a continuous renaissance in that kingdom. They supervise the elements and the seasons of our year. The law of cause and effect ordains the kind of ministry the earth deserves to receive. They cannot prevent earthquakes or floods, but they can bring rain or calm to a worthy region. Our careless neglect of soil conservation throughout the central states brought about many years of devastating dust storms. When humankind ignorantly or heedlessly commits an error, the Angels of Nature are not permitted to interfere with the accompanying compensation they attract in soil erosion. Were the great ones allowed to prevent such catastrophies, we would not learn our lesson concerning the right use and care of the blessings with which nature is endowed.

The Builders of Form, unlike the Angels of Nature, are

not in our atmosphere. The thoughts of these architects direct the planning and construction of manifestations that appear as new types of minerals, vegetables, animals, or persons. They work entirely from the fifth dimension, which is a realm devoted wholly to mental quests.

A colorful group of figures are the glowing Angels of Inspiration. Their auras are the shade of flaming sunsets, which contrast greatly with the contemplative serenity of their faces. Their intense feeling for beauty is expelled in vibrant thought forms they send earthward. These celestial impressions later appear in such melodic prayers as the opening strains of Wagner's *Lohengrin*. Inspired thoughts are entwined with the imagery of artists and poets that the ideal might be revealed as a beatitude. These divine dreamers may draw the spirit of a composer to their fervent levels or they might visit the sanctum of creative effort. The Angels of Inspiration seldom reveal themselves since they concentrate one-pointedly on the flow of lyrical ideas or harmonies reaching an aspiring individual.

The mystic announcement of sunrise sends forth a blessing before which all forms pertaining to the nature kingdom stand expectant and reverent. Resplendent colors mingled with the sound effects of the esoteric dawn herald the good tidings of a new day. Through the beauty of sunrise vibrate the incantations of the Angels of the Morning. They are emissaries from the Solar Logos whose task is to direct the spiritual radiations of the sun to this planet revolving before them.

The celestial workers who serve us directly and who keep nearer to us than most of the Angelic Orders are the Angels of Love. They are dedicated to the ministry of our guidance, healing, upliftment and harmony. Guardian Angels are beings who devote their time and efforts to our inner unfoldment. We do not attract the attention of these selfless ones until we are consciously seeking God's vast plan and purpose regarding us. When our yearning for self-conquest and wis-

15

dom grows intense, a Guardian Angel takes her place at our right side. Through her direction, understanding and overshadowing we are led to the various leaders and teachers we require for our inner training.

A Guardian is of great importance to our higher progress. The Guardian Angel stands next to the Master who is the teacher of our ray or path. Her advice speaks in our intuitions and her teachings in our deepening convictions. She leads us into the long corridor of overcoming, and when once within that hall of testing, she becomes our examiner and our initiator. As time advances us, the Guardian refrains more and more from counseling us. She remains with us during the lengthy process of our inner instruction, but at the first indication of our readiness to think and act independently, she withdraws her influence. Thereafter she remains with us as a protectress—a compass directing our footsteps. At any time our consciousness is clouded, hers is the clarifying current sweeping the mind of negative debris.

Guardian Angels are truly like patient, older sisters who uphold and direct us, and administer correction or encouragement whenever necessary. The strange ways in which they aid worthy charges is recorded in several instances in the Bible. In Matthew 1:20 an Angel appears to Joseph. Likewise, in Matthew 2:13 an Angel warns Joseph to flee into Egypt. In Acts 5:19, Guardians open a prison door; in Acts 12:7 an Angel releases Peter from prison. In Acts 27:22, an Angel warns Paul of shipwreck. The Bible makes numerous references to these loving servers whose faces are clothed with the radiance of those who know God. Guardians can be distinguished from other Angelic Orders by the golden radiation about the heart center, and by the pale pink auras which encircle them.

An interesting service is rendered by the Healing Angels. Theirs is the task of clearing the congested areas in our etheric bodies so that the flow of cosmic energies can affect the inner

A Guardian Angel

as well as the outer person. These workers are clothed in light blue radiations, and the color of the emanations from them signifies their service.

Hospitals and sanitariums are enfolded in the healing Light which these Angels create. The thought atmosphere about a place of suffering would be so heavy and dark that the finer powers could scarcely enter, were it not for the Healing Angels who, by their strong, pure, tranquilizing influence, equalize or change the surrounding atmosphere. They work for depression to be replaced by hope, and for pain to give way to peace.

There are at least three Healing Angels always about a hospital, but the prayers of individual patients or the devotions of anxious relatives often invite beings who accept single cases. They first ascertain whether a patient is to be released from the body, or healed. If their investigation reveals that the person's life span is not finished, they first arrest the illness and then work to enlighten the consciousness of the patient. They inspire doctors with the proper diagnosis and the right treatment. Whether a medical person prescribes or a metaphysician prays, help from the higher dimensions attends the afflicted. The coming new race, through telepathy, will be able to tune into the powers from the Healing Angels as assuredly as we now attune ourselves to our favorite radio program. Then the Angels will inform us of the obscure causes of our weaknesses, and with them teaching us how to heal the effects, we shall attain an unwavering healing consciousness.

The presences that enfold audiences wherever the Spirit of God is worshiped are called Religious Angels. These servants of devotion appear in a cathedral, chapel, hall or home when invocation is made to the Power of the Most High. When a chapel is empty, at least two workers remain to increase the silent influences of the church. During a service, however, each group attracts from three to twelve Angels whose delightful duty it is to utilize the devotional outpouring of the gathering. They direct these energies from the temple to the entire community so that passers-by not interested in religion will nevertheless receive an inner peace as they travel through these charged emanations.

During a service the Religious Angels strive to awaken passive persons into an active use of spiritual principles. The discouraged are relieved of their self-concern. Those searching for the Truth are given special guidance through a statement the minister or leader is impelled to utter. Were worshipers aware of the luminous figures above them, they would witness beauty impossible to describe. They would notice great faces peering down at them from billows of opal and coral diffusions. Time will open the heavy eyelids of our spirits that we may witness God's glory about us.

Occasionally we have heard about the "music of the spheres" without comprehending the full meaning of the term. In the Kingdom of the Angels exists an order consecrated to music. This order is not composed of an orchestra, but a choir. The songs are given out as chants; many of them are heard in march time. The magnitude of this choir is almost inconceivable; still more difficult to realize are the various octaves and keys in which this great assembly sings. Angels do not use vocal cords for speech or song. They speak from the mind and sing from the heart. When heard, their melodic variations are almost overpowering. The enthralling effects hymns of praise, courage, gratitude, love and worship have upon our world are very great. The ears of our inner self are always attuned to the Music of the Spheres. Our inmost selves are ever aware of the rhythmic cadences filling the higher dimensions, as natural to those realms as bird notes are to ours. All the experiences of humanity, Angels and God are expressed in these unending chants. Human composers have heard their songs depicting growth through struggle, the joyousness of

19

love, and the benediction of self-mastery. Their chants are directed to those laboring in factories, to those chafing in prison, to those who brave the anguish of pain. The sunrise hour of Easter attunes throngs to their triumphant praises. Alone, an individual aspirant in moments of stress, heroism or illumination is inwardly aligned with the chorus singing the anthem he or she requires for courage, balance or serenity. Though the reception of the heavenly music is seldom relayed to the conscious mind, the effects of the songs upon the inner self are noticeable by a surging and enlivening of the higher states of consciousness.

Were we capable of perceiving the Angels of Song, we would witness hosts of glorious singers whose auric emanations form a diverging rainbow of soft or bright hues, according to the tones of their songs. Wagner must have been very sensitive to the intonations of Angelic singers, for his scores reflect their songs quite clearly. Cesar Franck, a mystic of the arts, surely heard celestial overtones, for his music carries their transcendent message.

A glimpse of many Music Devas occurred while attending a symphony in one of Southern California's loveliest and largest outdoor amphitheaters. During the first selections of the evening a great number of Music Angels were visible, guiding the inner forces of melodic sounds into great streams of power which encircled the group. As the opening bars of Stravinsky's *The Firebird* were announced, a Great Figure enshrouded the multitudinous audience. In this one's radiations, everything seemed more alive, stronger and more enchanting. Never had music revealed its true meaning to me as clearly as it did while I listened enthralled that night. This glorious visitor affected others in the assembly too, as the enrapt people appeared singularly attentive. At the conclusion of the number the figure vanished. "Evidently," I remarked to my sympathetic companion, "that being was intent upon

An Angel of Music

helping to usher in new forms of music. The visitor must have been a masterly influence whose task is to bring us those harmonies that stir the intuitional qualities in each person. The novel number, *The Firebird*, contains the staccato notes that resound like knocking upon the gates of inner mysteries."

On our human pilgrimage, we are confronted by the supreme moments of birth and death. These passages are directed by beings of an eminent administrative degree. In size, beauty and development they are superior to the Angels already mentioned. The inhabitants of all the celestial dimensions are sustained by a peculiar inbreathing of that energy we call electricity. The Angels of Birth and Transition, like other Angels, understand how to inhale vivifying properties, but they possess an added capacity. They use electrical force to unite a soul with its infant body at birth, and to free the soul from its physical body at death. Only at these momentous junctures do we see the illustrious figures renowned for their wisdom, compassion and power. The last impression we have before we are plunged into the dimension of matter is that of a beatific face encircled by an aureole of blinding Light. The first presence to greet us as we cross the threshold of transition is that of the hallowed releaser. The wonders of birth and death are eclipsed by the momentary glimpses of the supernal pilots.

Beings from the celestial kingdom enter our kingdom, in human bodies, for various reasons. They are usually attracted by a curiosity to learn about those influences that enlighten us. Frequently those who enter our world are bewildered by our customs and routines. Consequently these visitors seem ill-fitted to our material world.

One of the most beautiful women of my acquaintance unveiled her origin to me by her illuminating comments. She remarked, "Though I have every reason to be happy with a devoted husband, lovely children, a beautiful home, and

An Angel of Birth

worthwhile friends, I feel imprisoned by my environment. In nature, I am like a bird freed from a cage. Throughout my associations with others and my reactions to material problems, I seem to see things as though I viewed them from the 'outside.' My husband and associates view situations as if they were looking at them from an 'inside' perspective. Am I unnatural? Should I learn to orient myself to their viewpoint?"

While the speaker had been analyzing herself, a flash of intuition enlightened me as to her identity. She was a Nature Angel, dissatisfied in this world. Slowly and carefully I explained my realizations to the anxious woman. Her eyes filled with the light of understanding as she said, "You have revealed the wellspring of my being. Knowing that I am a visitor here on a sacred quest will give me patience, tolerance and appreciation for the world I am visiting."

I am of the opinion that Marie Corelli, Olive Schreiner, and Vaslaw Nijinsky were beings from the nature line of evolution. A significant incident disclosed to me the homeland of the world's greatest dancer. On page 342 of the book *Nijinsky*, by Romola Nijinsky, is the account of a foot injury Nijinsky received. An X-ray unveiled the fact that Vaslaw's feet were not formed like that of other human beings anatomically; in fact they were a combination of human and bird construction. The doctor exclaimed, "This is the secret of his amazing elevation; no wonder he can fly; he is a human bird."

Occasionally beings from the celestial realms enter our dimension to perform some special service. This I believe, was true of Joan of Arc. There are times when the radiant ones find it necessary to give us help in concrete ways. Twice, while traveling, I had occasion to rejoice in their saving us from possible death. One foggy night, during my early childhood, my mother and I drove with a married couple through the Pocono Mountains of Pennsylvania. A flashing signal from my Guardian was a warning to the driver urging him to immediately stop the car. No sooner had he done so than a train whizzed past us. Sleepiness as well as the heavy fog prevented us from seeing the railroad crossing which was not clearly indicated. The four of us have never forgotten that night of grave danger and miraculous escape.

Years ago when on a lecture tour my husband and I faced sudden death on a busy highway. In the crucial moment we were conscious of a power that literally shoved our car into a soft snowbank. An exclaiming group of persons gathered, marveling at our deliverance. They found us deeply touched by this verification of invisible intervention.

Two very dear friends shared an extraordinary happening with us, trusting that we would understand its meaning more readily than they did. This middle-aged couple drove late one night through a desolate swamp region of Georgia. At this inopportune hour they had a punctured tire. Mr. G. searched uncertainly through his new car for tools. Unfortunately he carried no flashlight, which added to the strain of searching on a very dark night. It was finally decided that they would need help from some passing motorist who possessed a pocket light. The highway was devoid of cars when Mrs. G. suggested that they pray for help and protection. Although they had not seen a single car for more than an hour, they had scarcely opened their eyes when a touring car approached them. The driver of the car stopped and of his own will sprang lightly to the side of our grateful friends. The person who had volunteered his assistance was a young man who appeared tall, lean, and abounding in vitality and good humor. His significant greeting, "It is not safe for you to have trouble in this desolate place," later gave the couple reason for reflection. Without further remarks, the young helper busied himself about the car while Mr. G. held the flashlight brought over from the other car. Within a few minutes the youth said, "The car is now ready; you may be on your way."

25

Mr. G. extended a generous bill to the kindly youth. It was declined with the remark, "I have no need for that." When our friends were comfortably seated in their car, they were going to call out a friendly farewell to their rescuer when they suddenly realized there was no car and no person anywhere in sight. Two wide-eyed persons peered up and down the highway. "Why, that is odd," said Mr. G. "It is almost unaccountable! What do you suppose became of our knight errant? Perhaps he represented some special providence . . . I wish we knew." In hearing of this incident I recognized at once that the prayers of these two unselfish persons had attracted the attention of a willing server.

Intimate knowledge of the inhabitants of the Angelic Kingdom follows our longing for confirmation. The very fact that their existence is brought to our attention indicates a readiness on our part to enter the threshold of discovery. Before we can attain sight of crystalline levels, our consciousness must be purified, layer by layer. Sincerity, aspiration, and singleness of purpose, rather than chastity, dispel the fog of negative attitudes. The effort necessary to inner sight is not a matter of strength or determination, but rather of character development and a positive receptivity. These qualifications unfold through meditation and an exercise of the inner faculties in us.

To the aspirant, daily meditation is as essential as nourishing food. Regularity in this practice brings us a sense of an ever-widening consciousness. Meditation is the laboratory in which our Higher Selves are alchemists. One by one the baser elements in our interests and desires are transmuted, until the tone and movement of our energies follow an upward trend. By contemplating the joyousness and selflessness they know, our natures begin to reflect some of their Light, thus bringing us into rhythm with them. Each period of purposeful thoughtfulness deepens and enkindles our inner sensibilities.

The phases which receive our attention during meditation follow these general lines:
1. Devotion to the practice of self-mastery.
2. Perseverance in remembering the goal of our aspiration.
3. The practice of awareness.

The uncontrolled and uncultivated regions of our natures require daily consideration. Anger, intolerance and hatred weight us heavily with a gravitating influence. We must plan and carry out an elimination of destructive forces. Self-satisfaction, doubts and ignorance must be uprooted under our patient scrutiny. Measures should be taken for the mapping of our hourly overcomings. The price we pay in fruitful self-conquest is reasonable in comparison to the inestimable values we receive on our ascendant journey.

Should the discipline of our wayward thoughts and fancies seem arduous, our efforts can be reinforced. Reflection upon the luminous reality of Angels spurs us on to attainment. As freqently as possible we should take walks along unfrequented paths. Our being alone is essential. Before we embark upon an inviting trail, we should reflect. "This walk is dedicated to the recognition of God in everything about me. I will look upon all scenes with the realization, 'God breathes through these trees, from that mountain, and in the fields. God is the spirit that moves the birds to sing and the wind to croon.' I will be so occupied with watching and listening that should some presence enfold me, I will feel and see it, too." Then, as we leisurely walk, we are so filled by an attentiveness to the Highest that our own Infinite Selves look through the open door of our observation upon the world. Our minds are clarified, our emotions synchronized to the heartbeat of exultation, and slowly our physical sight is intensified by spiritual sight, and the countryside before us appears to be a gleaming spectacle of unimaginable beauty and life. There silhouetted against the brightness of this pictorial revelation are great, colorful beings whose slightest administrations express a vibrant, effervescent quality unknown to humanity.

With each advent into nature an enlarging conception and appreciation of eternal realities reawakens in us. The habit of awareness must be cultivated so that in any suitable place, in the home, in a garden, or in a temple, our consciousness can enter the higher kingdom enveloping us. When entrance to the vaster dimensions is made, our endeavor then consists of maintaining that awareness in all the departments of our lives.

What an infinitesimal fraction of the glories enveloping us do we ordinarily perceive! Sustained aspiration and constructive training will widen the circumference of our sight. Our realizations will include the limitless orders unfolding within the Pristine Spirit. How beautiful it will be to sense God in all Its manifestations! Wonderful, too, will be our joining the procession made of united humans and Angels whose reverent praises to the Highest reverberate throughout the universe.

An Angel of Prayer

NATIVES OF ETERNITY

THE ANGELS OF NATURE

Each of us is a recipient of gracious gifts that come to us hourly through the glories and favors of nature. We are indirectly influenced and enriched by the ministry of those shining presences that are called the Angels of Nature.

Everywhere we witness the work of this important group of Angels, for they keep the earth green, productive and beautiful. The wind, weather and landscape conform to their movements and directions. Even the transition of the seasons is influenced by certain orders who have charge of the quarterly changes.

Fluctuating about us momently are the Angels of the Elements. This group has many divisions, for all Angelic life evolving through the earth, fire, air and water kingdoms at some period serves nature. The Weather Angels are either Devas of Wind, Storm or Calm. The Angels of the Seasons each have their own way of vivifying or making dormant the life they protect. The Angels of Harvest hover over areas raising food necessary to the human race. One of our first realizations concerning nature is that certain localities are used as charging centers. Thus a virgin forest, a mountain peak, or a quiet lake might be the reservoir of great spiritual energy. One forest will be vibrant with healing energies which are especially invigorating to the etheric body. Another mountain fastness will possess a strong current of reverence for God. Lake regions are usually attuned to radiations of peace. The open desert country quickens keenness of mind. These contrasting vibrations are largely due to the types of beings which ensoul the various territories.

Occasionally when hiking in canyons or mountainous regions I have been attuned to the exuberant calls the Mountain Devas shout to each other across chasms or ridges. Every mountain chain has its directing Lord, as well as its numerous Angelic Guardians which are often called "The Spirits of the Mountains." These beings work toward stirring the languor of plant life into the activity of growth. In truth they are the impetus that quickens the lungs of nature. The sizes of these Guardians of the Summits vary from an average height of ten feet to that of a hundred feet or more. Nature Lords are as large as the mountains they enshroud.

When one with extended faculties enters the boundaries of Mt. Rainier National Park, the peals of resonant bells are heard which gradually diminish as one travels deeper into this renowned park. Imperceptible at first, and then with increasing clarity, radiations of deepest reverence are distinguished. Gradually the woodland spirits are seen, all traveling in one general direction. An atmosphere of complete devotion and veneration permeates the ongoing procession. Upon the higher elevations, three tiers of beings can be observed slowly moving upward, singing their hymns of praise in a great crescendo of celestial harmony.

At a point near the mountain peak, the nature spirits gather to stand in hushed awe before the altar of their Lord. As certain hosts conclude their adorations, they are replaced by those who stand behind them. Thus the processional of worship continues unbroken upon that majestic mountainside.

Overshadowing the snow-capped dome is the actual head and face of the Lord of Mt. Rainier. He turns slowly so that He may evenly bless all the areas over which He has charge. When the morning dawns, His face is toward the sunrise. By the afternoon He is facing the Paradise Valley area. There are no descriptions in the human language which can justly picture Him. But to one with extended vision His expression of serenity and compassion is unforgettable. The Lord of the Mountain is as understanding of human beings as He is of the Devas in His own kingdom. This is because He had incarnated in a human form.

Eons ago when civilization was still very young, this Nature Angel wished to incarnate in the human line of evolution. He keenly appreciated the value of human training for He came into a physical body in six successive lives. The principle which fascinated this particular Angel was the force we call love. Nature Devas develop joyousness in much the same way that love is unfolded by humanity. As the centuries progressed, the Angel who had taken these earth pilgrimages took the initiation of Lordhood which made Him a spiritual sovereign in His own kingdom. Now, because the Lord of Mt. Rainier understands human feelings, He greets every mortal who enters His aura with a ray of welcome. The whole of Rainier National Forest is a Nature Cathedral whose altar is graced by the presence of this One who has attained through fidelity and service to the Highest. These temple vibrations send their beams in every direction into those communities and cities which are nearby.

The Lord of Mt. Hood is a lieutenant under the Lord of Mt. Rainier and is one of the great Lords of Nature on the Pacific Coast. His great, benign face was in, not above, the mountain on the day that we traveled in that area. He sent His welcome in the form of a white shining ball, like a diamond, that was directed to the right-hand side (the receiving side) of the car.

The pointed lesson these sacred centers disclose is that the worship of God is natural in every kingdom. Even the builders of nature's forms are striving toward an attainment in consciousness and power which is exemplified to them in the Lord of Mt. Rainier.

Were we spiritually awake we should observe the verdure of the earth peopled by beings, exquisitely small and dainty, moving in harmony with the soft, diffused music of the heavens. Forests and mountains, thought to be lonely and uninhabited, would be known to be populated by many tall, graceful beings who hover over trees, lakes and hillsides. At all times of the day the happy Sylphs of the air would be discerned, busy in their lyrical activities above the countryside. Always at the high periods of the day—dawn, noontide and sunset—would the glowing Angels of the Sun be distinguishable on the horizon.

A Tree Deva is not beautiful according to our classical ideals of beauty as its features are too elongated and narrow, its face too triangular. Yet the Angels in charge of groves of trees have an excellent equivalent of beauty— boundless and eternal energy. They appear to be light green creatures, with flashing eyes that fairly bombard one with their vitality and penetration. Frequently Devas are as tall as the trees they overshadow, though they are usually much slimmer than the tree trunk. I have spent several hours, at various times, watching a Tree Deva move from tree to tree giving fully of its charging presence. Persons who love nature attract the attention and perchance a baptism of renewal from a Tree Deva. My

A Tree Deva

friends and I always make a pilgrimage to a certain tree on a beloved mountain because to us it is "the Giving Tree," or the tree with the welcoming Deva.

In learning of the vivacious presences who pervade the outdoors, ours is the joy of inviting them into our gardens. Where they are recognized and appreciated, gardens become more healthy and luxuriant. Ordinarily Devas do not enter busy cities, so the prana is very thin in such communities.

We are permitted to ask for their blessing or protection whenever we require it. In the past, my husband and I took yearly pilgrimages into pine forests to increase our communion with the Eternal. During these sojourns, the state of the weather was a very important matter to us. Some years ago dark clouds hovered over our camp very threateningly the evening we entered the forest. The postmistress, who knew us, worried about the durability of our tent as she wrote out a campfire permit for us.

Before retirement I went outside the tent and appealed to the Angels of Rain to spare our site. All that night we heard a heavy shower falling a short distance from us, yet our camp ground was not receiving any of that downpour. On our tour of inspection the next morning we found that the entire camp had been spared but the area that surrounded it, in circular form, was rain-drenched. The postmistress, in giving us our mail, scarcely believed us when we told her that the storm had not come upon us. I believe our call for protection enabled the Angels of Storm to promise us, "It shall not come nigh thee."

Rest days are very sacred to us for when they come we need their refreshment greatly. When on long lecture tours, free days usually come but once a month. One Saturday friends urged us to take our "day" with them

A Wind Angel

at their cabin by a lake. As the five persons in our party entered the closed-up cottage we realized that it would take too much time to unpack and dust the living room. We agreed that the cozy veranda was the best choice of a place to spend our time. As our luncheon was being taken out of baskets and placed on the table, a very strong, mischievous wind arose. Napkins and paper plates had to be weighted to prevent their escape. After our hostess placed us, the wind became so frolicsome that our hair threatened to hide our faces. We endured discomfort for a time and then I said, "Surely this wind can be calmed so that the day can proceed harmoniously. Together let us call upon the Angels of Calm to relieve the Angels of Wind about this place." All of us closed our eyes and sent out a mental entreaty for peace. No sooner had the last person opened their eyes than a great calm enveloped us. The estate at our right and the one to our left had leaves stirring everywhere. The lake before us was somewhat choppy, yet we ate our luncheon in freedom and spent an inspired afternoon together. In taking a hike we found that the Angels of Calm followed us, for wherever we went the wind suddenly ceased. Our friends were understanding and they rejoiced with us at this evidence of Angelic care.

Now we have made our home in a wooded canyon. Questhaven Retreat is situated six miles from the nearest village. The quietness and virgin atmosphere of this six hundred and fifty-five acre nature sanctuary affords splendid opportunities for study of the habits and duties of those Angels of Nature in this area. Extended vision has opened the door to the wonderland of realities that exist around individuals who make their homes in rural or wilderness regions.

It was while observing the activities of the many

Devas at Questhaven that we learned about King Tree Devas. In the oldest and largest live oak tree on the place is a highly advanced tree spirit, who was found to be the leader King of all the numerous tree Devas in the woods. He possesses a majestic quality of self-command, and the vitality he radiates has a stimulative effect on nearby growing things. A King Tree Deva strengthens the etheric bodies of the tallest and oldest trees in his immediate vicinity. Less developed tree spirits work on younger trees. On a few occasions the concise commands of the King Deva were heard. They were given in such a deep, resonant tone that their notes lingered in the woodland like a muted echo.

Until we lived at Questhaven we had not known that even Nature Spirits have their opposites with whom they evolve in loving harmony. The counterpart of this King Tree Deva, whom we have grown to love, is the Spirit of the Place. This order which gives service, protection, and contentment to a homesite is a feminine Nature Deva, whose ministrations bless the house, its people, and the entire property with spiritual renewal and physical guardianship.

The Angel of the Place makes her chief center in the atmosphere above a large tree near the Chapel of the Holy Quest. Here she is to be seen most of the time. However, since the entire grounds come under her charge, this gracious spirit can be observed moving from boundary to boundary, or from the flower garden to the distant beehives. It is this Constant Protectress who safefolds homes and land from destructive weather elements or unfriendly human beings. She also works upon the mental bodies of all whose thoughts need purification and regeneration as they enter her territory.

Questhaven's highest hill is named Inspiration Point.

Above its crest can be discerned the noble Guardian of the Summit. His is the task of guiding, blessing and instructing all those beings of younger evolution who are within his domain. The King Tree Deva is his assistant. The power which emanates from a Guardian of a Mountain is changeable. We have noticed that in certain periods of the day his blessings are peaceful. At high noon they become electric in potency, and even as his influence varies, so does his position. He is always facing the sun, so in the twilight we do not see his face. One beautiful summer evening while three of us walked reverently in the groves, the Guardian of Inspiration Point uttered this blessing, "Let all the earth be at rest—peace be unto everything." On another night he distinctly prayed, "Peace and sweet rest to the world."

A lovely mountain lies two miles to the south of Questhaven. There always seems to be a mantle of stillness surrounding it. We have called this mount, which is constantly aureoled by a lavender-blue radiation, Mystic Mountain. During the day the illusive, magnetic pull of this mountainside is felt by all our observant guests. When night falls, Mystic Mountain grows luminous on the higher planes. This inner Light attracts Nature Devas from near and far. Three Guardians stand at the entrance to the doorway of Light on the northern slope of the range. They see that none but those who are ready enter the open door into the ceremonies given wholly for Nature Devas. These rituals are in commemoration of the sun—a thanksgiving for the light and life received throughout the day.

At unexpected moments there come to our attention the silvery high tones of Angelic Choruses. Or we occasionally awaken to behold a day when nature is so clear and bright that inner world doors are widely open. The chief blessing of realizing the inner existence of all the Angelic lives is the inspiration they arouse in us through their selflessness, impersonality, beauty and devotion. Human beings are not God's only creation. To know something of His other orders expands the circle of our enlightenment. We live in wonder and praise of the Supreme Spirit Who made humanity and gave the Angelic Kingdom charge over us. Life's manifestations are multiformed, and each of its embodiments endeavors to reclaim the Light, beauty and harmony once known within the innermost.

Natives of Eternity

PERFECTED BEINGS AND THEIR TASKS

Life is a movement toward the goal of Mastership. An evolutionary program impels the advancement, improvement and mastery of ourselves and our talents. The supreme endeavor of progress is to cause every man and every woman to become Adepts in the art of spiritual advancement and the right use of spiritual powers. Though the process is slow and gradual, from the chrysalis of preparation, after tireless effort, a perfected man or woman emerges.

The treasures in knowledge these Masters gathered through various experiences and toil are the inheritance given younger souls still striving for wisdom and self-control. The benefactors, themselves, disperse their jewels; and their distributions cover an era of many centuries. In giving away the gleanings they earned by endless exertion, they thus enrich all the departments of human endeavor, and simultaneously become greater custodians of qualifications that entitle them to work within the estate of Eternal Power.

The group of Adepts who return their harvest to humanity are known as the Directors. They remain in inner communication with the earth, guiding its advancement in government, education, science, art and religion. Persons who, by their spiritual development, their devotion to world progress, and their special genius, merit masterly instruction and help, receive these advantages. How essential, therefore, are our aspirations which qualify us to work and grow under their supervision.

The Assembly of Masters seems sparse, indeed, until we consider the power invested in each Adept. Upon the advent of their Mastership, the majority of Perfected Beings enter the sixth dimension. In this region a service, which is vaster and deeper than the human mind can grasp, is rendered the Cosmos. It is sufficient to mention that the order and serenity in the universe is due partly to their united concentration.

The Great Ones who keep in touch with the affairs of the earth are the Directors previously mentioned, the Designers and the Initiators. These beings dwell in the fifth dimension, which to some is known as the Kingdom of Mind. In this region plans are conceived and prepared for execution. From here sensitive composers receive inspirations for melodic scores, while artists glimpse visions of beauty to reproduce on glorious canvases.

It is said by mystics that planets, stars and galaxies move in rhythm with the Music of the Spheres. This is true! The universe throbs with sound as fully as with life. In the outer world many creatures are articulate, but on the whole their notes are imperfect soundings. In the higher dimensions the quality of every tone is tuneful, upswinging. Waves of music flood one continually on the higher planes. There seems to be no end to their variations. At times they are silver toned and as distant as the far horizon. Again they are multisonous and resonant. Angels and human souls make up the invisible chorus of this permeating Spirit of Music. They do not gather in throngs to broadcast their harmony, but send out their tone or chant from their own sphere to add to the whole of the mighty chorale. There are beings, however, whose purpose it is to create concordant sound. They are the musicians and soloists whose adoration, through expression, forms the very soul of music. It is from the outline of their musical offerings that the world's finest works have been patterned.

When we attain realization of the Infinite Source of Life, we enter a training that prepares us for adeptship. From that time on we are under the supervision of Initiators who exert a high influence upon us. Under their watchfulness we are inspired with ideals and noble purpose. Their directions teach us to live usefully and progressively; yet, they do not solve our problems nor assume our responsibilities. Only by faithfully discharging our obligations and improving ourselves in body, mind, talent and spirit will we be able to sense their encouraging nearness.

There are seven major phases and gradations of initiation for the individual unfoldment of inherent Godliness. The first five phases are usually taken while in the physical body; the last two always occur in the higher dimensions of being. The term "initiate" applies to one who has achieved direct knowledge and consciousness of the Spirit of God. The depth of that inward realization determines the degree of initiation from which one functions in serving God's Plan. A *Master* has received the fifth initiation; a *Lord* has taken the sixth, while a *God* has concluded the seven great unfoldments of Godhood. The learned and spiritual men, Pythagoras and Lao-Tse, were Masters. The Christ Jesus and Gautama Buddha were Lords. The Bible refers to the *God*, Jehovah, Who, though exceedingly advanced, is not the Spirit of God to Whom we pray.

The Masters teach that Gods must take many

initiations before Their Spirits are united wholly with the Eternal Source.

Masters are supervised by Lords, and they in turn are overshadowed by the God of a particular way of unfoldment. Sixth degree initiate have the duty of radiating power, love and pure thoughts into space. Their attention is given to the Cosmos; Their help, to the world. Great Logi are so blended with the Spirit of God that They are channels of Deity's Thought, Benevolence, and Laws which direct the world. Though the journey from passivity to conscious Godhood appears difficult and complicated, infinite simplicity, order and wisdom govern the entire process. If the thought of graded orders of Mastership be confusing, remember that the Spirit of God permeates Its glorious system, that Its Life is in the leaves of the trees as well as in the hearts of human beings and Godly-aware Adepts. God is nearer than our bodies yet simultaneously pervades the universe. Only a Supreme Infinite Divinity could have fashioned a plan whereby all life would gradually evolve, until, from a sleeping state, eternal wakefulness might embody Its Creation. That the design be fulfilled, agents and artisans were necessary. Through long ages the most highly evolved humans have been the custodians of God's Intentions. Because these Adepts are essential to the purpose of the Creator, we should desire to know as much as is possible concerning them.

The earth is supervised by the Anointed Ones who either attained Mastery here, or who are responsible for the progress of this planet. The work of administration is shared by the Masters who serve in those fields best adapted to their abilities. The Adepts do not frequently reveal themselves or their services, for only a few of them and their ministries are known.

The Great Lords send us energy, inspiration and encouragement from Their high level. They seldom enter our dimension, as the Masters carry out their will for us. Amongst the Exalted Ones are the Lord Jesus, the Lord Maitreya, the Maha Chohan, the Sanat Kumara, and the Logos Osiris (the Solar Logos). Radiations from these Lords are felt very keenly on our Christmas and Easter Days, as well as during the full moon in May. The high noon period is a time when not only the Light but the silent benediction of the Solar Logos enfolds us.

The Masters in charge of the governments on our globe, about whom we know, are either guardians of nations, originators of systems, or distributors of power. The Master Ragoczy is overseer of Europe, though the various Adepts of each race assist Him considerably, The Master Morya helps direct the affairs of Asia. The director at the helm of these United States is called (after our country) the Master "Americus." His center of power has its unseen outlet over Lincoln Memorial in Washington, D.C.

The Adept called "The Conqueror" has the most strongly developed will power of all the Great Ones interested in governmental affairs. When a nation needs to arouse its capacity for self-defense or self-preservation, this Adept becomes the hidden power behind the country's transition. At present the Conqueror is overshadowing China, due to the necessity for this nation to overcome its lethargy. India will be awakened from her inertia by the same Director.

A peculiar duty is that of the Master Azabar who is in charge of monetary and credit systems throughout this world. Thus far, all mediums of exchange are of experimental origin. This Adept plans to inspire a system of exchange that will not engender the dangers of selfishness and monopoly of former systems. His plan cannot be executed until humanity admits a need for an improved method of exchange.

The best known Masters dedicated to the field of education are the Master Djwal Kul (also called The Tibetan), the Master Kuthumi, and the Master Elision. The Tibetan has charge of "organized thought," or established wisdoms and customs that need to be more thoroughly understood by the masses. The Master Kuthumi is devoted to the reception and spiritual radiation of the higher knowledge and trainings that are emanated in thought forms around this globe for sensitive minds or spirits to discern and utilize. The Master Elision is a woman of unusual attainment. She instructs persons who are to be sent into physical life as envoys with a particular message. Because of Her patient, serene instruction, new world movements or crusades are implanted in the fertile consciousness of souls preparing to incarnate. This imposing, beautiful Adept is sometimes contacted by Her pupils in the fifth dimension. Should these representatives forget their purpose, this Adept causes them to have an impressive dream or a spiritual vision which reawakens them to an awareness of their missions. Though there are many Adepts directing the investigations and enlightenments of science, the One best known to pupils who are in contact with Masters is the Master Hilarion. He remains closely in touch with our world to encourage and inspire, by thought, those individuals who labor to create the tools of progress. Two of the common subjects now occupying the concentration and efforts of the Master Hilarion are the cure of cancer and the wider expansion of the use of radio and television.

On the path of religion are the Lord Christ Jesus, the Promised Prince, the Master John, and the Master Quan

Yin. The Master Jesus took His sixth initiation by achieving "the ascension." Now, as the Lord Christ, He is the ruler of the spiritual impetus that is causing the inner awakenment of this humanity to an appreciation of eternal values. We have only been touched by the fringe of His influence, yet in this century alone the majority of those who love God have forsaken bigotry and intolerance for sincerity and tolerance. Under this Lord's guidance humanity will undergo many changes which will bring about an open-mindedness necessary for the awakenment of the spiritual powers in us. The Lord Christ is the One in whose keeping our spiritual welfare lies. With His assistant Masters, this Anointed One, who was recently Jesus the Galilean, is endeavoring to enlighten humanity, as well as to train living pupils for use in His Cause. Besides these services, His is the radiant Light which floods the inner worlds with a continuous stream of illumination and love.

The youthful Promised Prince, when seen, appears much like an artist's dream of the Boy Christ. This remarkable Adept has a merciful assignment—that of bringing about Divine intervention wherever it is merited. He is frequently felt, if not inwardly perceived, in those communities, cities or homes where tragedy stalks. When Adepts cannot avert wars, pestilence or violence caused by humanity's overpowering destructive thoughts, They influence us during the readjustments that follow chaos. The Promised Prince gives vision, courage, peace and gratitude to those whom His aura touches. In His presence children are happier, sweeter and more affectionate. We wonder what cause prompted this Adept to "spend His heaven doing good on earth." Our world is better for His ministry, and richer too, in spiritual contentment.

A great similarity exists between the Lord Christ and

His beloved disciple, who is now an Adept, the Master John. The resemblance is more of an inner likeness than an outer one. The Lord Jesus has dark bronze-colored hair, deep brown eyes, and is dignified in bearing. The Master John has honey-colored hair, blue eyes and seems boyish despite His attainment. Yet artists have confused these Great Men, and upon their canvases have put titles pertaining to the Christ, when in reality their painting was that of the Master John. A deep bond of eternal friendship between these two Anointed Ones has engraved upon the character of the younger Master something of the transcendent beauty of His Lord.

The Master John accepts earnest seekers of reality as candidates to be prepared for world service. The progress of the neophyte causes them to be a probationer, then a disciple, and later a pupil of Masters. During these stages of inner advancement, the aspirant may experience one or several spiritual illuminations, after which he is not only a conscious servant of Adepts, but also an initiate progressing toward Mastership. "The Holy One," as the Master John is sometimes called, educates every sincere seeker in the science of spiritual self-mastery. This Adept emphasizes that character development is the first requisite essential to higher mental and spiritual achievement. After disciples have gained self-knowledge and an honest attitude toward life, they are next enlightened as to how they may exercise the principle called *faith*, to free themselves from limitations in all departments of their experience. This develops one's inner powers in healing, as well as in the constructive acquirement of those qualities which attract love, trust, joy, prosperity and success. These forces remain as blessings only with those who share them with as many persons as they can enfold. The disciple ever realizes that "ceasing to share, we cease to have, for such is the law of love."*

The improvement of the aspirant's efforts, realizations, and successes fits them for the more difficult feats of inner unfoldment, which the Master John discloses to those worthy of further tuition. The Master John teaches that we are not in full possession of all our God-given senses. In the right season we are led to learn of the sixth and seventh senses which have their center in the realm of our spiritual being. The sixth sense records impressions that belong to octaves of light, sound and being beyond the third dimensional existence. The Great One believes "intuition," "clairvoyance" and "clairaudience" are terms that have been profaned by improper use, yet when truly understood, they are functions of humanity's innate sixth sense. The seventh sense is the faculty which permits the soul to withdraw from the physical body during sleep. It likewise functions whenever the Masters deem it advisable for conscious pupils to attend some inner conference, or take some inner initiatory work.

The Master John is but one of numerous Adepts who accept pupils. Others taking religious pupils, who are best known, are the Masters Lao-Tse, Amiel, Dratzel, Athena, Mohammed and the late Rama Krishna. The Adepts teach those under Their charge the principles which all Masters give to those who are worshipers of the Lord Christ. Yet, it must be remembered that all these spiritual conquerors are united by one endeavor—that of disseminating the radiance and principles of the Christ Spirit. This does not mean the doctrine the Christ Jesus gave in Palestine. The principles of the Lord Christ are far greater, vaster and deeper than those recorded in the Bible. To the fullness of the Christ message do these learned Masters bow.

*From Lowell's, *The Vision of Sir Launfal.*

In the East the Goddess Quan Yin receives loving homage because of Her mercy to the needy. This Being is really a Master who serves us universally from Her center in the higher dimensions. Her thoughts bring baptism and courage to the wretched in whatever state they may be manifesting. Serenely, modestly and compassionately the Master Quan Yin frequently enters our atmosphere to answer calls of distress. It is not the custom of this Illumined One to give attention to those who are joyous or happy, but rather to those who have lost their confidence and self-respect. There are no spiritual outcasts or souls unloved by God. The presence of such emissaries as Quan Yin proves how vast is the Infinite Love that envelops God's manifestation. However wrong the crimes or tragic the consequences, we find that sinners are attended by the same merciful observation given the Saints.

In the council of Perfected Men and Women is a department devoted to the subject of healing. Since the time of the Christ Jesus, the race has been urged to study and practice healing the body through the education of the mind and the strength of the spirit. Medical science, under the guidance of the Master Hilarion and His assistants, will continue its necessary work for the restoration of broken bodies. Yet, we are aware that healing can occur in the mind and spirit, but our approach to the inner healing fountain seems somewhat obscure. The Adepts who will be the exponents of our enlightenments regarding inner healing are the Master Dratzel, the Master Amiel, and the Master Mary. This latter Adept performs a great service through Her work in Lourdes.

The One who is teaching pupils the technique of spiritual healing is the Master Dratzel. He believes our illnesses are the result of our living contrary to the Divine

Laws of Rhythm and Equilibrium. Activity must be of the right tempo, otherwise there is strain and chaos. Periods of quietness, for the absorption of spiritual energies, are an essential requirement. When too much activity imposes itself upon our need of peace, our inward inhalation of necessary energies is prevented. In time the Divine Spirit's government of its body is dulled; later the mind becomes erratic and the emotions unsteady. Finally, on the physical plane we find a disabled body. The Master Dratzel is now teaching those pupils who are conscious of Him, that by at-one-ment with the Reservoir of Energy, by learning to absorb healing currents in nature's sanctuary, by sane living and intelligent eating, physical well-being is assured. To those who wish to understand more about the esoteric aspect of healing, the Master Dratzel's time is dedicated. The instruction consists of teaching humanity how to become a channel of restorative power, and how to conduct that knowledge and influence to those who ask for it.

The Master Amiel is a strong-minded Adept, though a gentle One. His task consists of inspiring spiritually-minded persons with the secrets of the laws of vibration and how they may be used constructively in healing. This art is for the priest rather than the physician; and the complete realization of this message cannot be attained in this age, for its full revelation belongs to unborn races.

Mary, the renowned Mother of Christ Jesus, is likewise an Adept. Her interests chiefly concern woman's emancipation from unnecessary physical suffering. By Her efforts more will be made to appreciate the wisdom of birth control, and of making birth a joy instead of a delirium of pain. The Master Mary represents the Divine element of Love, and as such She is a Master of all the

53

problems that confront women who faithfully fulfill the incentives of unselfish womanhood. Should guidance ever be required for the safety or welfare of the family life, the Master Mary is the One who will be attuned to the reception of that prayer.

The dreams and visions which weave themselves into poems, paintings and symphonies come from an exultant realm where joyousness, beauty and song are as natural to that sphere as mountains, plains and the sea are to this earth. The Master Serapis, surrounded by a host of Angelic Servers, stirs, quickens and uplifts our world by charging it with thought forms which sensitive individuals receive as inspiration. We open ourselves to be elevated by something expressed truly in thought, form or tone. The passion of the Master Serapis and His numerous shining collaborators is the worship of beauty and perfection in all the arts. Persons who are aspirants on this path should pray to the Eternal Source for creative power. The Master Serapis may be intoned by the invocation, "May Infinite Inspiration for the expression of beauty, melody or reality penetrate and illumine my consciousness."

The Avatars, who are leaders of the spiritual universe, communicate with their disciples on the earth chiefly through telepathy. When their presence is necessary in our world, they come in unassuming ways. They may appear at some diplomatic conference, disguised by a very ordinary body and manner. Thus did the Master Americus mingle amongst the group who inaugurated and signed the Declaration of Independence. Their purpose in appearances of this kind is to act as a silent but thoroughly imbued magnet whose force is directed toward the accomplishment of the matter at hand.

The pupils of the Anointed Ones confront many

situations of material and spiritual confusion which necessitate their control. In instances like these, certain Adepts will appear to their disciples, for the minds of the latter are apt to be too disturbed for the accurate reception of telepathic instruction. The beloved rector, Robert Norwood, had a visitation from the Christ Jesus, at a time of inner discouragement. The counsel of the Lord Christ, as well as the unusual inspiration of His sudden manifestation and disappearance, gave this minister the power and wisdom which made him a great and trusted man. Many are the accounts persons give who were recalled from death, who were mysteriously saved from accidents or from making wrong decisions, about a "vision" they'd had of the radiant Christ. The visions of others make all the more wonderful the actual appearance of an Initiate such as Robert Norwood experienced.

I, who write these words, do so in commemoration of a meeting with the Christ Jesus, which occurred in the high mountains. One summer morning, as I sat reveling in the beauty of nature, I heard human footsteps approaching me. Wondering who might be coming, I half arose to determine the visitor. The person I did see made me speechless, confused and unexpectedly timid all in one moment. The Man who came forward was partially hidden, at times, by trees or low limbs as He approached. Though I had frequently seen this Lord in His spiritual body, this manifestation was almost overwhelming. During the minutes that He spoke, I remained quiet, too reverent and inspired for outer speech. It is now many years since I heard that deep resonant voice, but were I blind, I'd recognize it anywhere in this vast universe. The Lord who advised me concerning the message I should give in His service, was extremely tall and very strongly built. His hair and short beard were of a bronze shade. His large eyes were a dark brown, and when He had gone, I remembered His loving but firm expression as appreciatively as I did the positive tone of joyousness and power which He vibrated. The spotless, loose white robe which He wore moved about His chest as He spoke and breathed, making me realize I was not seeing Him in a vision. At the conclusion of His instructions, He walked away as naturally as He had come. I leaned to the right to watch Him as He turned onto the road which hid Him from my view. At the time of His coming I greatly needed the strength and confidence of His orders. That strange appearance intensified my longing to bring others an awareness of the Great Ones. Words seem lifelessly inadequate when I strive to describe the transcendent glory of such a meeting.

The Masters are as varied in countenance and personality as are we who live upon this globe. The Promised Prince is a very handsome East Indian youth whose happy, loving spirit is contagious. The Masters Elision and Hilarion look like vibrant models of perfection in form. Both have wavy, chestnut-colored hair, fair skin, and blue eyes. The Lord Christ is best reflected to us by Hoffman's picture of Him, except for the sad expression the artist imagined. The Master Azabar appears more like a Westerner than a Chaldean which He was in a recent life. The Master Dratzel looks very Egyptian, for when He attained Mastership He was a high priest of Egyptian wisdom. This Adept's eyes seem black: they are piercing, probing eyes, whose influences are modified by the reserved, impersonal attitude of their possessor. In short, the Avatars look and speak like persons who were once human beings, but whose spirits were great enough to hold the lanterns of God's blessings in their services.

To individuals aware of the existence of Masters, all

days are purposeful. They may witness many incidents that reveal an unseen guidance or an unknown director of their affairs. Spiritual progress and circumstances combine their efforts toward the discovery of the Benevolent Mentor whose existence hourly becomes more perceptible. When Masters reveal Themselves to Their disciples, a companionship is begun which will brighten all the days of the aspirant.

Those who are already informed of the Masters they individually follow, in the process of their instructions from the Adepts, receive advice that is difficult to practice. For instance, the Great Ones reject our adulation for our respect and trust. In all relations with aspiring students, they emphasize that disciples are not to be dependent upon their Master, but upon themselves. The Illumined Ones should be considered as our learned and kindly Brothers and Sisters. Our attitude toward them should not be meek and worshipful, but confident and respectful.

The disciples' worship belongs to God; their honor and devotion to their Master; their aspiration to the exercise of the Christ Spirit within them. For such disciples, a day begins with the realization of God's Presence; it is motivated by service for the Master, and directed by the wisdom of the Adept's teachings. This training enables disciples to exert the growing powers of godliness and mastership that lie, otherwise unused, within.

Sincere students who yearn for personal confirmation as to the reality of the Masters, may do much to quicken their powers of spiritual awareness. It is surprising how much can be derived from the simple practice of thinking of the Great Ones the very first thing in the morning and the last thing at night. We must accustom ourselves to becoming "Master conscious." At high noon the influence of the Solar Logos, the Lord in charge of the sun, permeates our atmosphere and affects us strongly on the material as well as the spiritual planes. A loving, respectful salutation sent this Nature Lord greatly intensifies our reception of force from Him. In fact, the exercise of any reminder of the watchfulness of the Masters, such as periods of prayer, meditation or silence, will bring us spiritually into closer at-one-ment with them.

We cannot predict the exact moment pilgrims of reality will contact their invincible Director, nor whether they will see the Beloved Teacher or merely feel Their presence. If the time of communication could be foretold, it would occur during that period in which an aspirant's endeavors were wholly and unselfishly dedicated to the realization of God in Its universe.

It is not expedient that we follow the Masters in all their movements in order to learn of them. The seed we put into the waiting soil blossoms into flowerhood whether or not we understand the laws of nature that cause these changes. Gravitation continues its good service even though we seldom, if ever, think about its effects on us. The Perfected Men and Women whose loving interest blesses our planet and all it cradles, do not require our recognition. We are the ones who must awaken to the fact that there are Selfless Benefactors working invisibly and silently carrying out the will and plan of God. Ours is the privilege of learning of them, first through the experiences of others who have known them, and second, through our own unique realizations. Though they do not ask nor urge us to join the ranks of their ministry, we have the right to offer ourselves as servants to their Divine Cause. The greatest inward happiness we can attain is that of knowing we are one of their centers of usefulness over a great network of their guidance. May our joy in realizing the existence of Masters be such a transcendent, profound and renewing awakenment that its good will reverberate to the ends of the earth for the illumination and happiness of others.

NATIVES OF ETERNITY

INNER GLIMPSES OF LIFE BEYOND OUR PLANET

Adventures confront our explorers, the like of which have never before been conceived or achieved. The Earth's crust has divulged its hidden resources and its histories of earlier humanities. Sea depths have disclosed their strange assortment of colorful life. We now yearn to probe the mysteries of the heavens, for here lie treasures of knowledge entirely unprecedented in the field of discovery. Great telescopes and giant reflectors have been created because our world is interested in ascertaining the conditions of life beyond this planet.

On a clear night approximately five thousand stars are discernable to our naked eyes. How many of us have occasionally felt the fascination of starlit skies? In our survey of the celestial ceiling, our thoughts were possibly filled with questions and with wonderment. At such times a sense of kinship may have existed between us and the bright beacons of space. A few of us might have been bold enough to inwardly ask for an answer to our questionings.

Mystics, sages, and seers possessed a way of determining the information they sought concerning the star-studded universe. They knew of the presence of various solar bodies ages before the calculations or telescopes of astronomers revealed them. Their peculiar discernment was due to the development of the sixth sense, a faculty which is latent in every individual, though ofttimes unawakened. This sense enables one to transcend time and space since it allows an entrance into the higher dimensions of existence. This un-

61

usual faculty not only instructed the initiates, but it permitted them to travel, in their higher bodies, to the stars of their interest. Due to the activity of this inner power, Pythagoras predicted the appearance of certain heavenly bodies that were not known to humanity until the time of Galileo, and later, Newton. Today there are many persons on this planet who use the sixth sense as ordinarily as others use their eyes or hands. This faculty endows one with the power to investigate the realities of life without the aid of instruments or mathematics. As humans evolve, this power will be universally awakened and used.

Several years ago while in the high mountains our relation to other bodies in our solar system was revealed to me. That which followed this illumination answered all my inquiries about our starry neighbors.

One night while my companions were sitting around the campfire sharing their joys of the day, I was prompted to retire to a promontory that overlooked the surrounding sloping mountains. The night was the clearest of our stay in camp. The stars were so large and luminous that it seemed I might touch them if a giant bird were to carry me nearer them. Never before had I felt so at one with the star-flecked sky. My thoughts formed a torrent of questions. I reasoned, "Humanity might be the highest product to be evolved from the Earth, but is it the most highly developed creation in our solar system, or in the universe?" "Surely," I continued in my musings, "there are physical beings of much greater development than we've unfolded. I wonder which of the planets in our system has life similar or parallel to our own?"

Frequently had I pondered upon those questions, but not until this particular night did I feel that I must know. Inner challenges of this kind always bring results, and in ways quite unexpected, too. While inspiring thoughts were coursing through my mind, my attention was suddenly diverted by the appearance of an encircling Light, which illuminated the spot where I sat. Knowing this phenomenon as an announcement of a Master's presence, I slowly and reverently looked up into the face of the beloved Master, John. (This Adept took his mastership degree after his life in Palestine wherein he was the most devoted of the Christ's disciples.)

As nearly as I can recall, the conversation that followed began with the Master's explanation of His visit. After studying me a few moments, as though to analyze my inmost motives and longings, He said, "I have come to answer your questions. What can be explained to you will be done so, gradually, night after night at this very place. At times it will be necessary for you to leave your physical body so that you can travel safely with me to the planets of this system."

The Master John paused and as He did so, He turned His gaze from me to the heavens, so that during most of His instruction I watched His noble profile. The Advanced One continued, "Prior to our journeys to these bodies, you must know more about the relation stars and planets have towards each other. Everything that is issued in spheres of God-consciousness unfoldment comes in pairs as mathematical opposites. This is true of solar systems, of stars, planets and mankind. Regardless of the distances separating these expressions, a force of attraction continually exerts an influence between the two bodies."

The Master John glanced at me to perceive whether I fully understood his statements. I nodded affirmatively. When next the Master spoke, a note of love and gladness filled his tones. "The life-giving Sun has its opposite in a new star whose light has not been perceived as yet; call this body 'Elo.' When it will be observed it shall appear in the vicinity of Jupiter. Elo expresses the negative pole; the Sun, the positive. According to the Plan, Elo eventually will warm the planets of this system that now receive but little warmth from the Sun. When this manifests, the Sun, Mercury, Venus, and the Earth will have passed into oblivion.

"The Sun and Elo have their cosmic brothers and sisters. The stars with missions similar to that of your own stars are Rigel and its opposite, Vega; also Sirius and Capella. A high comradeship, undreamed of by human beings, exists between these friendly luminaries."

The planets, so familiar to you by name, have their division according to the pole of energy they represent. Thus we find:

POSITIVE	NEGATIVE
Mars	Mercury
Earth	Venus
Jupiter	Saturn
Uranus	Neptune
Pluto	Vulcan

My complete interest was given this Masterly Visitor so that the minutes seemed as seconds to me. When the Master paused longer than usual I knew He in- tended to leave. His deep blue eyes regarded me intently when He spoke. "Ponder upon what I have told you. Keep your own counsel in respect to these revelations. When the season for sharing this knowledge approaches, you will be informed. Selah!"

In rejoining my companions I was greeted by loving, eager inquiries. "What happened to you upon the mountain? You look as though you had seen the Master." "I did see one of the Lord Christ's Assistants, the Master John," I replied. "He cautioned me to be silent about His instructions until given permission to speak. I received much tonight that is going to revolutionize my entire conception of the cosmos."

Expectant faces scanned mine hopefully, but I held my peace. One of the members thoughtfully declared, "It is not necessary that we know what was revealed. We are included in the spiritual radiance of that message, for have you not all noticed how charged our atmosphere has been during the last ten minutes?"

The others had felt the tremendous power that surrounded us. "Goodnights" were more softly and sacredly given that evening than previously.

The following night I awaited the coming of the Master with a joyous heart. I had not been in meditation but a few moments when the sudden burst of Light announced His

Presence. The Master used no idle words in needless greetings. Addressing me in a kindly but positive voice, He began: "Prepare to leave your physical body, in the way you have been taught. Tonight you are going to make a solar excursion to the moon."

The Master John aided me to put my physical body in a relaxed but consciously "awake" state. As I "stepped out" of my material body, the lightness, harmony and energy of the mental body I found myself using was exhilarating. The Master's right hand clasped my left hand and in that manner we traveled through all these experiences. His power and guidance thus protected and enlightened me constantly.

Hardly a minute elapsed between the Adept's clasping my hand and my next realization of actually being within the atmosphere of the moon.

Our view of the satellite was similar to that which passengers have in airships when about five thousand feet above terra firma. However, the panorama upon which we looked was devoid of any sign of life. We looked upon a bas-relief composed of extinct craters, some of them in plains, others on hills or mountain tops. Mentally I compared the scene before us with a desert wasteland, dotted by great mountains rising unexpectedly out of nowhere. Yet it was not sand I saw below, for the Master explained that it was more like baked clay than any other substance with which I was familiar.

The Master John encircled the globe and wherever He paused for me to note the scenery it was always dry wastes that greeted our eyes.

During all the time we spent in studying the surface of the moon, I was conscious of the most eerie sensation, which indicated a force entirely foreign to me. I could not see what caused these peculiar radiations. The Master read my thoughts for He said, "You discern a strange magnetism pervading us. The source of this pressure you feel is the only thing of interest on this dismal cosmic island. Listen carefully.

"In every solar system a place is always created that will receive the exiled Nature Spirits who misbehave while working in those planets that have physical life upon their surfaces. The Nature Kingdom is governed by a moral code wholly unlike that which governs human beings. Exile from the mother planet is not planned for the purpose of punishing mischievous beings who become destructive, but for balancing them and teaching them gratitude for their path of evolution."

Many questions were prompted by the wise Adept's statements. I felt the Master wished me to express them. Immediately I asked, "Do the offending Nature Spirits ever return to the planet they once served? If they return are they better for their exile?"

The Master answered: "When the misdirected impulses are reconverted into constructive energies, then releasement from this 'island' is gained. The beings who were treated here for balance, progress steadily and happily throughout the remaining courses of their evolutionary progress on their native planet."

"Why do the etheric beings who inhabit this body generate such a peculiar aura of power?" I inquired curiously. There was something unnatural in the emanations from this place.

"The exiled creatures existing here are deeply grieved, unhappy or homesick when they first find themselves on this satellite. The selfless Guardians who teach the Nature Spirits gradually dispel the dark aura of depression about these beings. Yet the unquenchable longing of the spirits for their native planet creates a field of magnetic yearning whenever they center their thoughts upon their homeland."

The Master John took me so close to the exterior of the moon that we were but three feet or so above it. I wondered what would now be forthcoming. The Great One gave an inner command and suddenly the atmosphere was teeming with Nature Spirits. They were not accustomed to visitors, for their inquisitiveness and desire to see us almost alarmed

66

me. With relief I perceived that the Master had erected an invisible barrier so that they were unable to come nearer than twenty feet to us on all sides. For many minutes I was occupied in observing these strange creatures. I observed earth, air, fire and water representatives. Close to me were a sylph, a tall tree deva and a fire sprite. The wave of yearning I felt from these spirits was almost unnerving. Seldom have I been as profoundly moved as by these creatures' need for love and sympathy. While I watched the few hundred spirits before us, the Master John addressed them, giving them inspiration, courage and vision. Knowing the differences in language and expression between the nature and human kingdoms, I was impressed by the fact that this varied assembly understood with one accord. Telepathic transmission disclosed the Master's thought images which could be comprehended by any order of life.

After the close of the address the whole group and satelite vanished instantaneously and I found myself on the high knoll which overlooked the campfire my friends enjoyed nightly. The Master had not given me a parting instruction, but that was unessential for I had His guidance and His revelations to reverently cherish.

The persons who accompanied me to our hallowed retreat respected my silence pertaining to the nightly lessons. Everyone was aware of a great and high vibration that enhanced and ennobled our lowliest tasks. I longed to share the unusual teachings which were enriching my knowledge, and on several occasions I almost answered the questions I heard others ask concerning conditions on the moon. Little did I dream that it would be almost four years before I was permitted to speak about these inner discoveries.

On another evening I was inwardly saying, "What will it be tonight?" My eagerness and happiness again necessitated a supreme effort in disciplining my emotions so that they would be poised sufficiently to afford me temporary releasement from my body.

The golden light which nightly blessed the trysting place

gave evidence that the Adept instructor had come. The Master regarded me with a smile as He said, "In reply to your mental question—it shall be Mercury tonight."

The new planet we observed attracted us, like a mystical magnet, until we were almost near enough to walk upon its sandy surface. From various perspectives we noticed the same sandy contours. On the physical plane Mercury was a parched desert with no sign of life whatsoever.

The Master broke our silence, "Due to Mercury's close proximity to the sun it cannot support physical life, yet in a moment you will witness the lives it does sustain with the reflected inner light from the sun." Hardly had the Adept ceased speaking when a sudden flash of lightning caused us to see into the etheric sphere enshrouding Mercury.

Innumerable emotions coursed through me as I gazed in amazement and then in reverence at the beings around us. These were representatives of the fire kingdom and what vivid, energetic and glorious creatures they were! Some appeared to be like tall brilliant tongues of flame. The bodies of many Mercurians were saffron-colored, while others resembled pale gold. From the smallest shining fire elemental to the great Lords of Flame, joyousness, vitality and purity radiated.

Ascending into their dimension we perceived that these beings lived in unusual cities created by their thoughts. They appeared to be similar to large, stately towers. Except for such characteristic dwellings, the scenery was mostly composed of brilliant colors which draped the inner world of Mercury in cloud effects. To me, this was indeed another world, unlike anything I had ever seen. I felt intensely drawn to the majestic inner world which pervaded this arid planet.

"Mercury is really an island of the Gods," said the Master, reading my thoughts. "The Lords of Flame, who govern all the fire elementals in this solar system, meet their emissaries on this small globe. There are Lords existing within this atmosphere whose service is so vast and inclusive that should They cease Their ministry, this system, lacking plan-

A Lord of Flame

etary guidance, would whirl chaotically into space. Many of the Fire Guardians leave Mercury when such bodies as Pluto require their elements. The Fire Angels ray out their creative force which influences musicians, artists or writers who possess the necessary sensitiveness . . . Thus can you understand how infinite are the varieties of Servants the Eternal God uses in the distribution of His power."

Upon my return to my body that evening I reviewed all that had been said or shown to me, for I considered this solar journey very important. I felt a new kinship toward the fire beings as I sat several minutes before the campfire, hearing my friends discuss the day's unfoldment.

For several nights I was taken by this Adept to visit far off places that I had only gazed up into the stars before to realize. As we traveled inwardly to each planet to uncover its inner purpose and plan for unfolding life physically and etherically, I was filled with a sense of heartfelt gratitude to the Master Designer of the universe. While much of the life I witnessed is intended to remain in God's vast mystery, I was allowed to share some of these revelations to help each of us lift our gaze into the greatness of the Divine that flows throughout the Cosmos.

Though my association with the Adept was solely for enlightenment, and though no personal messages were imparted to me, I realized that in His care and guidance I found more joy than I might ever have gleaned from friendly salutations.

The following day as I thought about the Master John's visit that evening, I intuitively realized He would then conclude His instructions, at least for the present. Because of this realization His last visit was all the more stirring and impressive.

"I see that you do understand how interrelated are the stars and their dependent bodies," He began, "the joy of the Supreme Ruler grows stronger as His creations recognize and salute each other. One of your inner practices should be a daily consideration of those bodies we have visited as well as of those Planetary Lords whose radiations your planet receives."

Spontaneously I interrupted, "Master, I know so little of the Planetaries, please tell me what is necessary to realize of Them."

A look of veneration increased the inner beauty of the Master as He spoke of His Superiors. "Planetary Lords are of various degrees of advancement. The Supreme Lord of all Planetaries rules the empyrean of space from the star Altair. This 'Great Master' of the Universe directs the formation and dissolution of stars and their complementaries."

"Under the Lord of Altair are such Planetary Lords as the Director of your Sun (Osiris). Every star is governed by a great Lord of Fire, who in turn guides the movements of the Planetary Beings whose outer bodies are planets. These Beings evolve and relieve Those above Them of Their duties, thus emphasizing how endless and eternal is progress."

Again I interrupted, "Master, should we seek to communicate with these advanced Rulers?"

The Master's reply was, "If, in your meditation and silence periods, you endeavor to send out love or greetings to these Lords, They will respond by strengthening your spiritual powers. They can draw us to Them, in spirit, but we are only able to attract Their attention and constructive radiations. I advise you to salute the Sun Lord daily at high noon. This is a suggested salute, 'The Christ power within me attunes me to Thy radiations, O Solar Logos. May I be receptive to Thy charging and Thy strengthening currents of Divine energy. I recognize Thee, Father of this solar system, and the Christ within me salutes Thee.' "

The Master turned in a circular manner so that His gaze included the host of blue beacons in that summer night's sky. "Whenever possible, praise and bless the heavens at night," the Master instructed. "This invocation is inclusive and beneficial, 'May Divine Love attune me to my universal and planetary sisters and brothers.' "

I knew the Master was now to leave. My mind tried to

71

phrase a fitting remark of my deep gratitude, but words seemed superficial in His presence. My heart cried "Thank you, Master, for revealing a new Heaven and a greater Earth to me." By His nod of loving assent I realized that He understood even more than I had believed, the full extent of my gratitude.

In the days that followed I established a telepathic link with all the important solar bodies the Master had taught me to appreciate. To me the universe was no longer unbounded space; it became a canopy of throbbing life, and more, I knew a deepened faith in the Power and Presence of the Silent God, whose dominion includes all that which ever has been, which is, or ever will be. The Love behind the galaxy of luminaries exerts Its influence in distances undiscovered by our sciences, but it likewise pervades those lives within our perspective, the unfolding flower, the bird in flight and the unending progress of Humankind.

Estarius, the "Great Mother"

This Great One sends out her power from the star, Altair. Her love and guidance flow to every planet in the cosmos which cradles life. Once a year this 'Great Mother' envelops our planet consciously. This Sacred Overshadowing always occurs during our fifth month.

Natives of Eternity

ANSWERS REGARDING HIGHER BEINGS

In the years following the initial writing of this book, Flower A. Newhouse was asked many questions to not only clarify but deepen one's understanding of the glorious hosts of ascending Forms of the Infinite Creator that are ever growing Godward. What follows is a collection of questions she was asked, followed by her response:

Question : What proofs are there for the average person to recognize that the Angelic Kingdom and the Hierarchy of just and pure souls made perfect in God are true?

Answer: Humans with carnal desires and mediocre habits cannot know some of the highest and the most sublime truths, because they are totally unqualified to benefit from such knowledge. Insensitive persons and those with great skepticism are beings whose own inner darkness prevents them from seeing the Light.

However, all through the centuries, in every land, there have been sensitive and aspiring individuals whose nobler thoughts and living qualified them to realize the existence of Higher Orders. The old and new testaments of our Bible contain incidents of men and women who were ready to know something about the extensions of higher consciousness. Even in our own time there are persons whose higher faculties and whose living enable them to be aware of other orders of existence. The fact that most human beings are blind and insensitive to higher realities does not discredit the testimony of those who possess sight and realization.

Question: Are the Masters to be considered divine or are they to be honored as advanced souls?

Answer: They are to be honored as Great Souls. Remember, though, They have achieved perfection. They have achieved what humanity is responsible to attain before being finished with the earth.

Although advancing souls need not come back to earth to take their fifth degree initiation (mastery), they keep coming back until achieving sainthood, which is the third degree of initiation. But the most valorous will return after the third initiation in physical bodies, and therefore their development will be faster. The time will come when they are perfected. Masters live as members of the great Hierarchy of Just and Pure Souls Made Perfect in God. They live very apart from humanity. They do not want people to depend on them personally, and when They make entrance into our life, They will do so at some experience of illumination. But more often an experience of enlightenment is precipitated by the Christ and by His great Christ Angels.

And so, it isn't until you get into the Inner Worlds that you really know much about the Great Ones called the Masters. We honor Them. I reverence Them, but not in the way I reverence the Christ and They would not have that. They want the Christ to be known as the greatest soul that has ever lived.

Question: Why doesn't God bring humanity to perfection instantly instead of having us go through lifetimes of trials and testings since we will ultimately be one with our Creator anyway?

Answer: Don't forget, every one of us has to earn every blessing, every reward, every element of growth that we face. God's purposes, which function through the long slow way of evolution, are indicative of the patience that is required of our own soul in relation to our ongoing and our unfoldment and our ripening spiritually. Never let us be so childlike as to imagine that in the twinkling of an eye a great Lord or God would bring us to perfection. We would lose the adventures of growing, overcoming, and transcending if others were to do work that is wholly and completely our own.

Question: Why do Masters not live more among humanity? Is Their influence stronger on the higher levels?

Answer: Masters are among the highest fruit of civilization. It is no more extraordinary that They do not live among people commonly, than it is that doctors of philosophy and of law do not teach our kindergarten and elementary grades. There is a season when the student's mind is ripe and prepared for training by wise ones. This is true, too, of a person's spiritual faculties. When inner maturity is developed, we may expect to aspire to the expert tuition of the Masters of Humankind.

Until we are inwardly ready for higher instruction, the guidance of these High Initiates comes to us through the broadcasting of Their Powers throughout the spiritual dimensions.

Question: How may we best serve the Higher Ones?

Answer: We need to become more still, more at peace within—truer centers of maintained power. Restless waters cannot reflect the glories of the Overshadowing Presences; only still water mirrors Eternal Powers. The Master John advises channels who are awake to be centers of deliberate calm; to attain undisturbed peace in a very vital way through meditation and then to send forth this influence of calm into the atmosphere of the planet. It shall be of greater power than many prayers.

Another way in which to serve is to ask, at night, to be taken to those centers or areas of Light where teaching or counsel is to be given by Initiated Ones. Very seldom do we ask definitely before retirement for this specific guidance. Another way is to ask to work with the Master Mary and her Host of Angels of Love in such a way that we become magnets, drawing Their beams and carrying healing currents.

Question: Do Masters know of Their past lives?
Answer: All Masters are aware of Their past. For instance, the Master Elision realizes she was once Hypatia, and the Master Hilarion was Leonardo da Vinci. The Master Elision and the Master Hilarion followed the path of evolution that everyone follows. It was usual for Them, as it will be for all of us, to have three or four outstanding lives in which They gave service to humanity. Before these times of world service were achieved, They knew a long evolutionary period wherein character and intellect were steadily improved.

Question: Could you tell us any more about Quan Yin?
Answer: This is the Chinese and Japanese goddess of mercy. There is actually a presence who is Asian in appearance, a very wonderful feminine soul, who has this office. She works with the fourth aspect of the deity—the Spirit of Grace. The love and radiance of this glorious soul function and work through this outpouring of God.

Question: Can you tell us more about the Master Elision?
Answer: This Great One is dedicated to teaching esoterically. She is a second ray Teacher, and would be particularly interested in revealing to humanity the future of life, and the archetype of the new races. She is able to impart knowledge concerning ourselves and our Divine Life Plan. This Master meditates upon light waves and sends Her instruction into

the world through this medium. Her ministry is very similar to that of the Master Koot Hoomi, Who is also a second ray Adept.

Question: If Jesus were all-powerful, why could He not have revealed the truth of Immortality in a way less tragic than the crucifixion?

Answer: The Drama which the Christ enacted so gloriously necessitated His elimination of humanity's fears of pain and death. He bore these tests and triumphed that we might take heart and, from His symbolic example, find strength to challenge the negative aspects of life to develop their constructive aspects in us.

Question: What became of the Lord Maitreya when the Master Jesus became a Lord?

Answer: The Lord Maitreya, who formerly filled the office of the Christ, is now completely free of our planet and has returned to work in the sphere of Venus from whence He came. I do not believe, as is stressed by some esoteric groups, that Jesus is now living in a physical body in Syria. I believe, because I have heard it from the Lord Jesus Christ directly, that He is the Lord Christ, filling now the same office that the Lord Maitreya formerly filled.

Question: What is the meaning of the term, "The Cloud of Silent Witnesses," mentioned in the New Testament?

Answer: This term refers to those highest forms of evolution from every way of life—Angelic and human, as well as those lines of life which are as yet unknown. This "cloud" is really composed of Lords, Logi, Seraphim, Cherubim, Thrones, Dominions, Principalities, Virtues, and Powers who are able to venerate the Supreme Spirit unbrokenly even while engaged in the Tasks of Their ranks.

Question: What is the Being in charge of present humanity called?

Answer: The One Who has charge of this present humanity is called "The Lord of the World." He is mentioned in our literature as "The Sanat Kumara." Of course, over Him is the Great Planetary Logos, Who is the Exalted Ruler of the planet, but Who does not preside over the detailed government of this world.

Question: Is our Soul and Guardian Angel the same thing or are they separate entities?

Answer: Indeed they are different entities. Our Soul is part of our Higher Self and has been with us even before our physical bodies were first formed. Therefore our Soul is very ancient and it is very worthy of being called our Higher Self. But it is not the Guardian Angel. The Guardian is much more unfolded than most people are to the influence of their Soul as yet; much more aware of life and knowledgeable, and certainly able to help us more proficiently. The Soul in most people is rather sleepy and only in the advanced person does it become awake and active and instructive. And as soon as the Soul takes over and sends forth, as it were, messages, lessons into consciousness, then the Guardian speaks less to us because we are getting it from a source that is pure and high in our own Divine Self.

Question: How does a Guardian Angel "choose" her charge?

Answer: A Guardian chooses someone She has overshadowed and assisted while being a Watcher Angel. She may have had one hundred or more souls She watched over previously. From this cluster She selects one for whom She has the greatest hopes or for whom She feels the most deeply.

Question: Does a Guardian Angel eventually make Her Presence known to her charge?

Answer: As individuals advance in consciousness and training, they begin to perceive a guiding, helpful Presence. This assistance is most discernible during times of danger or emergency. From this dim sense of a Higher Presence, awareness and knowledge of this Invisible Protector grows. The time will arrive when the full realization of this Angelic Benefactor is achieved and maintained.

Question: How can one call on their Guardian Angel?

Answer: Always preface any call to Angels or Masters with the phrase: "In Christ's Name, dear Guardian Angel, bring into my consciousness the wise decision for this matter at hand. God bless and make ever more fruitful my efforts in Christ's Name." Or you might ask, "In Christ's Name, dear Guardian, let me know and realize, beyond my own endeavors, the mantle of Your deep protective care." Or again, you might say, "In Christ's Name, Blessed Guardian, quicken in me a realization of the innermost values of this lesson and help me to understand this testing that I may meet it victoriously."

Question: How may one come to recognize and render due reverence and gratitude to those Beings who are giving humanity instruction and guidance for the realization of growth and the deepening of consciousness?

Answer: It is wise, whenever you are free to do so, to look up in consciousness. Your Guardian Angel is usually near, so look up and thank her and smile. You should remember your Guardian as your spiritual mother. On the outer plane you know how greatly interested your mother is in anything you do, and in anything you conquer. Your Guardian's interest is a thousand times greater than that of your outer mother whom you love and honor. She will be made most happy by your growth, and every time you overcome a negative habit or attitude Her growth will be quickened. "In the Christ's Name it was done and also for love of you," is a statement appropriate to your Guardian Angel.

Question: After reading about Angels I felt attracted to Music Devas even though I am not a musician. Would one who loved music, but who was unable to play a musical instrument, ever attract these Beings?

Answer: Your deep appreciation for good music would make you receptive to the radiations from Music Devas. Their emanations might at any time start a flow of creative ideas within your being which could result in a song, a tone poem, or a theme for an epic work. All these ideas, to one untrained in music, would require the expert and willing collaboration of those skilled in this art. Regardless of your age or talent, if you are able, learn to play some instrument; for this will not only enrich your enjoyment of music, but it will result in a stronger bond between you and the Music Angels.

Question: How do Religious Angels work with groups who have gathered for worship?

Answer: At such times, Angels are in constant motion. Thought waves from those in meditation go out; also waves created by hymns, prayers, songs, and rituals. The Angels dip into these waves, molding and focusing their strong radiations upon persons who need their beneficial influence. Every group that mentions God is like a bonfire, attracting Angels to use its channelship for increasing the recognition of God.

Question: Can you explain why so often I smell the incense of sandalwood?

Answer: St. Bartholomew voiced a truth when he mentioned that he noticed Angels exhaled fragrances. Angelic

Beings can be distinguished by Their fragrances. Healing Angels emanate that which is similar to the scent of pine forests. Guardian Angels give us impressions of an inspiration lovelier than any of our flower perfumes. Sandalwood must denote a Presence who works either along healing lines, or along the lines of creative instruction.

Question: The terms Deva and Angel are used interchangeably, so that I am confused as to where the Nature Kingdom ends and the Angelic Kingdom begins?

Answer: In esoteric literature the term Deva refers to a being who is evolving through service to the Nature Kingdom. Devas take spiritual initiations just as human beings do, but theirs are more numerous and of a kind wholly different from those of human individuals. When Devas advance to a certain degree of attainment, They are called Angels. After They have completed the training of Angelhood, They pass into a vaster consciousness and service and are then designated as Archangels. They also achieve other ranks above the Archangel level.

Question: (a) What colors do Tree Devas emanate? (b) Do they teach or help humans? (c) Are they found in all trees, in the city as well as in the country? (d) Is it possible to converse with them?

Answer: (a) Normally, all Tree Devas have light green emanations; but that is because we usually see them on the astral level.

(b) Tree Devas are not particularly teachers to human beings. In fact, it would be an exception of the rule for them to be so. There are other Angelic Orders who might fill this role but not Tree Devas—others, such as Guardian Angels, the Angels of the Christ Presence, the Angels of the Christ Host, and the Angels of the Order of St. Michael.

(c) You will find Tree Devas in all large trees, whether in

the city or outside. The difference between the high mountain Tree Devas and the city Tree Devas would be that the former work solely for nature's renewal whereas the latter have had much contact with humans and therefore may be able to strengthen human beings in special ways with their vital emanations through the trees they energize.

(d) Realize that a Deva Presence activates the trees about you. Select a specific tree as the particular tree of your observant regard. Whenever you pass the tree, send it love. In time, you should receive intuitional responses from the Presence within the tree. Were it possible for you to sit beneath this tree for any length of time, you would probably note certain currents coursing into your aura. These are the "heartbeats" on the etheric level of the tree's Spirit. Anyone who is sensitive to them is blessed and remagnetized.

Question: Do Nature Spirits work with plants within the city?

Answer: Yes, they are active wherever there are green growing things though not in as large numbers as in the countryside. The most advanced ones who desire to do so are able to come into the cities to work, but the younger beings remain in the more remote places along with Advanced Devas who choose to stay in the great outdoors.

Question: What causes one to feel, while looking at Crater Lake, that it does not belong to this earth? It seems ethereal.

Answer: It is an abode of advanced Nature Devas whose emanations are never disturbed by the presence of human beings.

The Planetary Logos of Venus

Made in the USA
Las Vegas, NV
06 May 2023

71659602R00052